DNA Don't Lie

By

D. Edwin Easter

LEGAL DISCLAIMER

This book is for educational and informational purposes only. It does not constitute legal advice and does not create an attorney-client relationship. Laws vary by jurisdiction and change frequently. Readers are encouraged to verify all information with their local court rules, statutes, or a licensed attorney before acting on any legal matter.

LIMITATION OF LIABILITY

The author and publisher disclaim any liability for loss, injury, or damages incurred as a result of the use or reliance upon the information contained in this book.

Acknowledgement

This book would not exist without the many people whose support, patience, and belief carried it from an idea to these pages.

First, I acknowledge the truth itself — often uncomfortable, often inconvenient, but always persistent. DNA Doesn't Lie is rooted in the conviction that facts matter, science matters, and integrity matters, even when the truth challenges long-held assumptions.

To those who shared their stories, experiences, and insights: thank you for your courage and trust. Your willingness to speak openly gave this book its human depth and purpose.

I owe immense thanks to my family and close friends for their patience and unwavering encouragement. You sat beside me through long hours of research, writing, and revision, reminding me why this work mattered when the process felt overwhelming.

Finally, to the readers: thank you for your curiosity and openness. My hope is that this book challenges you to question, to learn, and to trust evidence over assumption — because DNA doesn't lie, and neither should we.

Dedication

To the truth — because evidence speaks when words fail.

About the Author

D. Edwin Easter is a pro se legal author dedicated to empowering individuals who must navigate the justice system without an attorney. Drawing from firsthand experience and extensive independent legal research, he writes practical, plain-language guides that break down complex court procedures into steps real people can follow.

His work focuses on paternity challenges, child support disputes, and the realities of legal fatherhood—areas where misunderstandings and procedural missteps can have lifelong consequences. Through his writing, Easter seeks to equip readers with the knowledge, strategy, and confidence to advocate for themselves in court, while understanding both the power and the limits of pro se representation.

Table of Contents

CHAPTER 1

When the Truth Changes Everything

Discovering through DNA testing that a child you believed was biologically yours is not, can feel as though the ground has been ripped out from under you. For many men, this revelation arrives years after an emotional bond has formed—often after legal obligations have already been established. The shock is not only personal; it is legal, financial, and psychological.

This moment is not just about biology. It concerns status, rights, obligations, and procedures.

The legal system does not automatically undo paternity simply because DNA proves non-parentage. In many states, paternity is as much a *legal construct* as it is a biological one. Understanding that distinction is the first step toward regaining control.

This book exists for one purpose:

To help you navigate this situation without a lawyer—pro se—using knowledge, procedure, and lawful strategy.

You are not alone. Thousands of men face this exact situation every year, often with little guidance and even less sympathy from the system. What separates those who remain trapped from those who successfully challenge paternity is not money—it is **timing, documentation, and procedural literacy**.

Let's look at some different scenarios-

Scenario One: You Signed the Birth Certificate, Believing the Child Was Yours

Signing a birth certificate is not a ceremonial act—it is a legal declaration. In many jurisdictions, this signature creates a **presumption of paternity** that is equivalent to a court order.

Common Misconception

"If DNA proves the child isn't mine, everything automatically stops."

This is false.

In most states:

- The birth certificate establishes **legal fatherhood**
- DNA alone does **not** undo that status
- A court order is required to disestablish paternity

What This Means Pro Se

If you signed the birth certificate under the **reasonable belief** that you were the biological father—and later discovered fraud, mistake, or misrepresentation—you may have grounds to challenge paternity. However, courts often impose **strict time limits**. Delay can permanently bar relief.

Key legal concepts often involved:

- Voluntary acknowledgment of paternity (VAP)
- Fraud, duress, or material mistake of fact
- Equitable estoppel (the court prioritizing the child's stability over biology)

Understanding these doctrines helps you frame your case properly rather than emotionally.

Scenario Two: You Are Paying Child Support Under a Court Order

Many men discover non-paternity only after years of child support payments. This is one of the most legally complex and emotionally charged situations.

Hard Truth

Even with DNA proof:

- Child support does not automatically stop
- Arrears often continue to accrue
- Refunds are rare and heavily restricted

Courts typically distinguish between:

- **Prospective relief** (ending future obligations)
- **Retroactive relief** (recovering past payments)

Most jurisdictions allow only the former, and only after proper filing and hearing.

Pro Se Strategy Focus

Your goal is not outrage—it is **procedural correctness**:

- Filing the correct motion or petition
- Attaching admissible DNA evidence
- Requesting relief, the court is legally allowed to grant
- Avoiding arguments, courts routinely reject

Men who lose these cases often do so because they argue on moral grounds rather than on legal grounds.

Scenario Three: You Were Married at the Time of Birth

Marriage introduces one of the strongest legal presumptions in family law:

The marital presumption of paternity.

In many states:

- A husband is presumed the father regardless of biology
- This presumption can override DNA evidence
- Courts may refuse to disestablish paternity entirely

This scenario is prevalent when:

- The mother had an affair
- The truth emerges after divorce
- The child already knows you as "dad."

Legal Reality

Courts often prioritize:

- The child's emotional continuity
- Established parental bonds
- Public policy favoring stability

Pro se litigants must understand that biology may carry less weight than **timing and relationship history**.

Scenario Four: You Acted as the Father Without Knowing the Truth

Some men never signed a birth certificate or court order but functioned as the father:

- Lived with the child
- Held themselves out as the parent
- Provided support voluntarily

In these cases, courts may apply doctrines such as:

- De facto parenthood
- Psychological parent theory
- Equitable estoppel

These doctrines can bind you to obligations **even without biological or legal paternity**, primarily if the child relied on your role.

Pro se success in these cases depends on:

- Clear timelines
- Evidence of deception or concealment
- Demonstrating lack of informed consent

Scenario Five: You Discovered Non-Paternity Early

This is the strongest position to be in.

If DNA results surfaced:

- Before a court order
- Shortly after birth
- Within statutory rescission periods

You may have significant leverage to:

- Rescind acknowledgment.
- Prevent support orders.
- Avoid long-term legal attachment.

This chapter later explains how to act quickly, preserve evidence, and avoid procedural traps during this critical window.

Why the System Feels Unfair—and What You Can Do About It

Family courts are not designed to determine "truth" in the emotional sense. They are designed to:

- Protect children from instability.
- Reduce public assistance burdens.
- Enforce procedural finality.

Understanding this removes confusion and replaces it with strategy.

The court is not asking:

"Is this fair to you?"

It is asking:

"What does the law allow us to change, and when?"

Your power as a pro se litigant comes from learning how to speak the court's language.

Moving Forward

This book does not promise easy answers or guaranteed outcomes. What it offers is **clarity**, **structure**, and **realistic options**. Each chapter builds toward one goal: empowering you to act deliberately rather than react emotionally.

You did not choose this situation—but you can choose how you respond to it.

Knowledge is leverage.

Procedure is protection.

Timing is everything.

In the chapters that follow, you will learn how to:

- Assess your legal posture honestly.
- Gather and present evidence correctly.
- File the proper motions at the right time.
- Avoid common pro se mistakes that permanently close doors.

This is not about revenge.

It is about **restoring order** in a system that rarely explains itself.

CHAPTER 2

Legal vs Biological Fatherhood

One of the most misunderstood concepts in family law is the difference between **biological fatherhood** and **legal fatherhood**. Many people assume that DNA controls everything. In reality, **the law does not always treat biology as controlling**, and in many cases, biology becomes legally irrelevant once specific actions or deadlines occur.

Understanding this distinction is critical. Countless men lose their rights, money, and legal standing not because the facts are against them, but because they misunderstand how the law defines "father."

The Core Distinction

There are two separate concepts at play:

Biological Father

- Determined by genetics and DNA testing
- Answers the question: *Who actually conceived the child?*

Legal Father

- Determined by law, court orders, or legal acknowledgments
- Answers the question: *Who does the law recognize as the child's parent?*

These two roles **can be the same person—but they do not have to be**.

How You Can Be the Legal Father Without Being the Biological Father

It is entirely possible—and common—for a man to be:

- **Not the biological father**, yet
- **Still the legal father** under the law

This usually happens when one or more of the following occurs:

- You signed the birth certificate or an acknowledgment of paternity
- You were married to the mother at the time of birth
- You failed to contest paternity within the legal time limits
- A court entered a paternity or child support order naming you
- You acted as the child's father for a significant period of time

Once legal fatherhood is established, **DNA alone does not automatically undo it**.

Why Courts Do Not Automatically Follow DNA

Courts are not truth-seeking laboratories. They are **institutions of order and finality**. Judges are trained to protect systems, not emotions.

When paternity is challenged after legal fatherhood has already been established, courts prioritize three core principles:

1. Stability of the Child

Courts focus on what disrupts the child's life the least. If a child has known you as their father:

- Financially
- Emotionally
- Legally

The court may decide that changing paternity causes more harm than maintaining the existing arrangement—even if DNA says otherwise.

2. Existing Legal Relationships

Once a legal relationship is created:

- Parent-child rights attach
- Support obligations attach
- Custody and visitation rights attach

Courts are reluctant to undo these relationships because doing so can create uncertainty, instability, and administrative chaos.

3. Finality of Judgments

Courts value finality. If a judgment could be reopened anytime new information surfaced, **no ruling would ever truly be final**.

This is why:

- Time limits matter
- Procedures matter
- Missed deadlines matter

The law rewards those who act **early and correctly**, not those who act late but are emotionally justified.

Biology vs. Law: An Uncomfortable Truth

The legal system does not exist to guarantee biological accuracy. It exists to:

- Resolve disputes
- Assign responsibility
- Protect reliance interests

In many jurisdictions, the law assumes:

"A child is better off with a legally responsible parent than no parent at all."

As harsh as it sounds, courts sometimes view legal fatherhood as a **status that can be accepted, waived, or lost**, independent of genetics.

Common Misconceptions That Hurt Pro Se Litigants

Many self-represented litigants make fatal assumptions, such as:

- "Once I get a DNA test, everything will be reversed."
- "The truth will matter to the judge."
- "Fraud automatically voids paternity."
- "I can raise this issue anytime."

These assumptions are often wrong.

Courts usually ask:

- *When did you know or suspect?*
- *What actions did you take?*
- *Did you challenge paternity within the statutory window?*

If the answer is "no," the court may refuse to hear the DNA evidence at all.

Why Procedure Matters More Than Emotion

Family court is not about fairness in the emotional sense—it is about **process**.

You can be:

- Morally right
- Factually correct
- Genetically excluded

And still legally bound.

This is why **procedure matters more than emotion**. Statutes, deadlines, and prior orders constrain judges. They cannot simply "do what feels right."

Pro Se Insight: The Law Cares About What You Did, Not What You Feel

If you are proceeding without an attorney, understand this clearly:

- The court will examine **your legal actions**, not your pain
- Your credibility depends on timing, consistency, and filings
- DNA is evidence—but **only if the law allows it to be considered**

Legal fatherhood is not undone by outrage. It is undone—if at all—by **strict compliance with statutory procedures**.

Why This Chapter Matters

Before you file anything, argue anything, or emotionally confront anyone, you must answer one question:

Am I challenging biology—or am I challenging legal status?

Those are two very different battles, fought in very different ways, with very different odds.

Understanding the difference may determine:

- Whether your case is even heard
- Whether relief is legally possible
- Whether you are permanently bound despite the DNA

CHAPTER

3

Signing the Birth Certificate What It Really Means

For many men, signing a birth certificate feels like a formality—something you do in the hospital, under pressure, in the middle of an emotional moment. Few understand that this single act can create **permanent legal consequences**, even if DNA later proves the child is not biologically theirs.

In most states, signing the birth certificate or executing a **Voluntary Acknowledgment of Paternity (VAP)** does far more than record a name. It can establish **legal fatherhood** with the same force as a court order.

1. Birth Certificate vs. Voluntary Acknowledgment of Paternity (VAP)

Although often discussed together, these are legally distinct concepts:

- **Birth Certificate**: An administrative document used to record parentage.
- **VAP**: A legally binding document in which a man formally acknowledges paternity.

In many states:

- Signing the birth certificate **is treated as signing a VAP**, or
- A VAP is executed simultaneously at the hospital or shortly after birth.

Once signed, the law typically presumes:

- You knowingly accepted legal fatherhood
- You waived the right to demand immediate DNA testing
- You agreed to assume parental rights and obligations

This presumption exists **even if no biological testing was performed**.

2. Legal Effect: A Presumption Equal to a Court Order

A properly executed VAP often carries the **same legal weight as a judicial determination of paternity**.

That means:

- You may be ordered to pay child support
- You may be listed as the legal parent in court records
- You may be barred from later denying paternity without court action

Courts rely heavily on VAPs because they promote:

- Administrative efficiency
- Stability for the child
- Finality in family law matters

Once entered, the burden shifts **to you** to undo it.

3. Why Courts Enforce These Documents So Strictly

Courts are not primarily concerned with fairness to adults. Their focus is on:

- **The best interests of the child**
- **Stability and continuity**
- **Avoiding disruption of established parent-child relationships**

As a result:

- Emotional distress, betrayal, or deception alone is often insufficient
- DNA evidence may be ignored if raised too late
- Courts may prioritize the child's reliance over biological truth

This is why many men lose paternity challenges **even after definitive DNA results**.

4. Challenging a Signed Birth Certificate or VAP

Despite how final these documents appear, they **can be challenged**—but only under specific conditions.

Common legal grounds include:

- **Fraud** (intentional misrepresentation)
- **Duress** (coercion or pressure)
- **Material mistake of fact**
- **Lack of informed consent**
- **Improper execution or defective form**

However, the availability of these arguments depends heavily on **timing**.

5. Timing Is Everything

Most states impose strict deadlines to challenge a VAP or birth certificate:

- **Short rescission period** (often 60 days or less)
- **Extended challenge period** (often 1–2 years) but only for limited grounds
- After deadlines expire, challenges may be barred entirely

Once the statutory window closes:

- DNA evidence alone may no longer matter
- Courts may rule the issue "settled."
- Legal fatherhood becomes permanent by operation of law

This is why delay is often fatal to a case.

6. The "Best Interests of the Child" Barrier

Even when fraud or mistake is proven, courts may still deny relief if they find that disestablishing paternity would harm the child.

Factors courts may consider:

- Length of time you acted as the father
- Emotional bond with the child
- Whether another man is available to assume legal responsibility
- Financial reliance and stability

This doctrine can override biology entirely.

7. Signing Without DNA: A Critical Mistake

One of the most damaging assumptions men make is the belief that they can "fix it later."

Legally:

- You are presumed to have accepted the risk of uncertainty
- Failure to demand DNA testing before signing is often viewed as a waiver
- Courts may treat later objections as buyer's remorse

The law assumes adults understand what they sign—even when reality proves otherwise.

8. Pro Se Warning: Hospitals Do Not Explain This

Hospitals and staff are not required to explain:

- The long-term legal consequences
- The loss of future defenses
- The difficulty of reversal

Many men sign:

- While exhausted
- Without legal counsel
- Under emotional pressure
- Based on trust rather than proof

The legal system rarely considers these circumstances sufficient to set aside the document.

9. Key Takeaways

- Signing the birth certificate or VAP can create permanent legal fatherhood
- It often carries the same weight as a court order
- It can be challenged—but only under strict rules
- Timing and legal grounds are critical
- Biology alone does not control the outcome

Understanding this chapter is essential because **what you signed may matter more than what DNA proves.**

CHAPTER

4

DNA Testing-When the Truth Comes Too Late

DNA testing is often viewed as the ultimate truth. Scientifically, it is. Legally, it often is **not**.

Many men discover—sometimes years later—that a child they are legally responsible for is not biologically theirs. They believe DNA will automatically correct the record. What they soon learn is that **timing, procedure, and prior legal acts matter more than genetics**.

This chapter explains why DNA evidence frequently fails to undo legal fatherhood—and what can still be done when it does.

1. DNA Proves Biology, Not Legal Status

DNA testing answers only one question:

Is this man the biological father?

Family courts ask a different question:

Should this man remain the legal father?

Once legal fatherhood is established—by birth certificate, VAP, marriage presumption, or court order—DNA becomes **secondary evidence**, not controlling authority.

Courts routinely rule:

- Legal paternity ≠ , biological paternity
- Biology alone does not undo legal obligations
- Stability outweighs genetic truth

2. Why DNA Evidence Is Often Rejected

Courts commonly reject DNA challenges because of:

- **Statutory time limits**
- **Waiver by conduct**
- **Estoppel**
- **Best interests of the child**
- **Finality of judgments**

In plain terms:

If you waited too long, acted as the father, or signed documents accepting responsibility, the court may deem the DNA test legally irrelevant.

3. The Legal Doctrines That Block DNA Challenges

A. Waiver

By signing a VAP or birth certificate without demanding DNA testing, courts often rule you **waived the right** to contest paternity later.

B. Estoppel

If you:

- Held the child out as your own
- Provided financial support
- Established a parental bond

The court may estop (block) you from denying paternity—even with DNA proof.

C. Res Judicata / Finality

If paternity was established by court order, the issue may be legally closed.

4. When DNA *Can* Still Matter

DNA evidence may still succeed if:

- You act **within statutory deadlines**
- You prove **fraud, duress, or material mistakes**
- The child is very young
- Another biological father is identified and available
- No long-term parent-child bond exists

DNA is strongest when paired with **procedural compliance**.

5. State-by-State Variations (Grouped Overview)

Strict Deadline States

(Short windows, harsh enforcement)

- Florida
- Texas
- California
- New York

Common rules:

- 60 days to rescind VAP
- 1–2 years max to challenge
- DNA alone is insufficient after the deadline

Moderate Relief States

(Allow limited post-deadline challenges)

- Ohio
- Michigan

- Pennsylvania
- Illinois

Common rules:

- DNA admissible with fraud or mistake
- Best interests analysis still applies

DNA-Friendly States

(Statutory disestablishment procedures)

- Georgia
- Alabama
- Tennessee
- Missouri

Common rules:

- Specific statutes for paternity disestablishment
- DNA required
- Must meet procedural steps precisely

Warning: Even in DNA-friendly states, missing a filing requirement can destroy your claim.

6. Case Law Examples (Illustrative)

Case Example 1: DNA Rejected Due to Delay

A man challenged paternity six years after signing a VAP. DNA excluded him.

Court ruling:

Challenge denied. The man acted as the father, missed statutory deadlines, and the child relied on the relationship.

Principle: Timing outweighs truth.

Case Example 2: DNA Accepted Due to Fraud

Mother knowingly misrepresented paternity. DNA excluded the legal father—action filed within the statutory window.

Court ruling: Paternity vacated.

Principle: Fraud + prompt action can overcome presumption.

Case Example 3: Best Interests Override DNA

DNA excluded the father, but the child was 9 years old and had no other father figure.

Court ruling: Legal fatherhood maintained.

Principle: Child stability overrides genetics.

7. Pro Se Checklist: Before You File Anything

✓ Obtain certified DNA results (court-admissible lab)
✓ Identify how paternity was established
✓ Check your state's challenge deadline
✓ Determine applicable legal grounds
✓ Confirm child's age and relationship history
✓ Identify whether a biological father exists
✓ Gather proof of fraud, coercion, or mistake
✓ Prepare for a "best interests" argument

8. Pro Se Checklist: Filing Strategy

✓ File motion under correct statute or rule
✓ Attach DNA results as exhibits
✓ Request evidentiary hearing
✓ Address best interests proactively
✓ Cite statutory authority

✓ Avoid emotional arguments
✓ Meet all service requirements

9. Motion Template: Motion to Disestablish Paternity

IN THE [_____] COURT OF [COUNTY, STATE]

[Your Name],
Petitioner

v.

[Respondent Name],
Respondent

MOTION TO DISESTABLISH PATERNITY

COMES NOW the Petitioner, pro se, and respectfully moves this Court for an Order disestablishing legal paternity, and states as follows:

1. Petitioner was previously adjudicated or presumed the legal father of the minor child.
2. Newly obtained genetic testing excludes Petitioner as the biological father.
3. Petitioner files this motion within the statutory time allowed OR based on fraud/mistake.
4. Petitioner did not knowingly waive the right to contest paternity.
5. Continued enforcement would be inequitable and contrary to justice.

WHEREFORE, Petitioner requests:

- Disestablishment of legal paternity
- Termination of future child support
- Amendment of vital records
- Any further relief deemed just

Respectfully submitted,
[Your Name]
Pro Se
[Address]
[Phone]

10. Motion Template: Motion for DNA Testing (If Not Yet Done)

MOTION TO COMPEL GENETIC TESTING

Petitioner requests court-ordered DNA testing pursuant to [state statute], stating:

1. Paternity is contested.
2. No prior court-ordered genetic testing occurred.
3. Testing is necessary to determine biological parentage.

WHEREFORE, Petitioner requests an Order compelling genetic testing.

11. Key Takeaways

- DNA proves biology, not legal fatherhood
- Courts prioritize procedure over truth
- Deadlines control outcomes
- Fraud and timing are critical
- Pro se litigants must act precisely
- Delay is often irreversible

The tragedy is not that DNA comes too late—It's what the law warned you, but never explained.

CHAPTER 5

Time Limits, Deadlines, and Statutes of Limitation

Procedure beats truth when deadlines expire.

Every state imposes strict time limits to challenge paternity—whether paternity was established by signing a birth certificate, a Voluntary Acknowledgment of Paternity (VAP), an administrative order, or a court judgment. These limits are often short, unforgiving, and rigidly enforced. **Missing a deadline is the single most common reason courts deny relief**, even when DNA conclusively proves non-paternity.

This chapter explains **why deadlines exist**, **how they differ across pathways, which exceptions may apply**, and **how to protect your rights pro se**.

1. Why Time Limits Control Paternity Challenges

Courts prioritize:

- **Finality of judgments** – the law disfavors reopening settled cases
- **Stability for the child** – emotional and financial continuity
- **Administrative efficiency** – preventing endless litigation

As a result, the legislature imposes statutes of limitation and procedural deadlines that often override biological truth.

Key Principle: DNA answers the question of biology. Deadlines answer the question of law.

2. The Three Most Common Paternity Deadlines

A. Immediate Rescission Period (Usually 60 Days)

Most states allow a short window—typically **60 days**—after signing a VAP or acknowledgment of paternity to rescind **without cause**.

Characteristics:

- No need to prove fraud or mistake
- No DNA required
- Simple rescission form or motion
- Often administrative, not judicial

After this window closes, paternity becomes legally binding.

Many men mistakenly believe the birth certificate itself is harmless. It is not.

B. Extended Challenges Based on Fraud, Duress, or Mistake (2–5 Years)

Once the rescission period expires, most states allow challenges only if the petitioner proves:

- Fraud (intentional deception)
- Duress (coercion or pressure)
- Material mistake of fact (belief you were the biological father)

Common Timeframes:

- **2 years** in stricter jurisdictions
- **3–5 years** in many states
- Measured from **date of acknowledgment**, not date of discovery

Higher Burden of Proof:

- DNA test
- Affidavits
- Documentary evidence
- Credibility findings

Courts frequently rule: *"You should have known sooner."*

C. States Allowing Challenges at Any Time (Limited & Conditional)

A minority of states permit challenges **without time limitation** when:

- DNA conclusively excludes paternity, **and**
- The petitioner acts promptly after discovery, **and**
- No strong parent-child bond exists, **and**
- The challenge serves the child's best interests

These statutes are **narrowly construed** and **rarely applied automatically**.

3. Statute of Limitation vs. Statute of Repose

Understanding this distinction is critical:

- **Statute of Limitation:** Clock may start at discovery
- **Statute of Repose:** Absolute deadline—no exceptions

Many paternity statutes function as **repose statutes**, meaning:

Even fraud does not stop the clock.

4. How Courts Calculate Time (Common Traps)

Courts typically calculate deadlines from:

- Date of signing acknowledgment
- Date of entry of judgment

- Date of administrative order

Not from:

- Date of DNA test
- Date you "found out."
- Date mother admitted the truth

Emotional discovery ≠ legal discovery

5. Tolling Doctrines (Rare but Possible)

Some courts recognize limited tolling for:

- Concealment of fraud
- Lack of notice of proceedings
- Minor child status (rarely helps fathers)

Tolling is discretionary and uphill. Never assume it applies.

6. Interaction With Child Support Enforcement

Even if paternity is later disestablished:

- Past-due child support (arrears) often remains enforceable
- Refunds are rare
- Enforcement continues until court orders otherwise

Time limits apply separately to paternity challenges and support modification.

7. Pro Se Deadline Survival Checklist

A. Emergency Deadline Checklist (Use Immediately)

Identify **how paternity was established** (VAP, birth certificate, court order, admin order)

Locate the **exact statute** governing paternity challenges in your state

Determine whether the statute is a **limitation or a repose** statute

Calculate deadlines from the **date of signing or judgment** (not discovery)

File a **protective motion** before any deadline expires

Request court-ordered genetic testing if not already completed

Request a **temporary stay** of child support enforcement

Serve all required parties (mother, state IV-D agency)

B. Evidence Assembly Checklist

- Certified copy of acknowledgment or judgment
- DNA test results (AABB-accredited if possible)
- Affidavit explaining date and manner of discovery
- Evidence of fraud, mistake, or misrepresentation
- Proof of prompt action after discovery
- Prior child support payment history

C. Filing & Procedure Checklist

Correct the court with subject-matter jurisdiction

Correct case caption and case number

Filing fee or fee waiver request

Proper service per the rules of civil procedure

Calendar response and hearing deadlines

8. Sample Motions and Language (Pro Se)

A. Motion to Disestablish Paternity (Filed Within Statutory Time)

COMES NOW Petitioner, pro se, and respectfully moves this Court to disestablish paternity pursuant to [State Code § ___], and in support states:

1. Petitioner executed a Voluntary Acknowledgment of Paternity on [date].
2. Petitioner has since obtained genetic test results excluding him as the biological father.
3. This motion is filed **within the statutory time period** permitted by law.
4. Continued enforcement would result in manifest injustice.

WHEREFORE, Petitioner requests that this Court disestablish paternity, terminate prospective child support, and grant all other just relief.

B. Protective Motion to Preserve Deadlines (Before DNA Results)

Petitioner files this protective motion to preserve statutory rights pending genetic testing. Failure to file before expiration would permanently bar relief, regardless of test results.

C. Motion to Order Genetic Testing

Petitioner respectfully requests court-ordered genetic testing pursuant to [State Code § ___], as genetic parentage is directly at issue and necessary for adjudication.

D. Motion to Stay Child Support Enforcement

Petitioner moves for a temporary stay of enforcement pending resolution of the paternity issue, as continued enforcement may result in irreparable harm and unjust enrichment.*

9. Strategic Guidance

- **File first, test second** when deadlines are close
- Assume courts will strictly construe statutes
- Never rely on verbal assurances or equity arguments

- Treat every paternity case as a **race against the clock**

Delay is denial.

10. Case Law Illustrations: Deadlines Trump DNA

These cases reflect a consistent national trend. Titles and principles are provided for educational purposes.

A. Fraud Alleged — Relief Denied as Untimely

In re Paternity of Cheryl, 746 N.E.2d 488 (Ind. 2001)

The court held that even intentional misrepresentation by the mother did not toll the statute. The father's motion was denied because it was filed outside the statutory window.

"The statute reflects legislative intent to favor finality over biological certainty."

B. DNA Exclusion — Still Too Late

Robert J. v. Leslie M., 51 Cal.App.4th 1642 (Cal. Ct. App. 1997)

Despite conclusive DNA evidence excluding paternity, the court enforced California's statutory deadline and denied relief.

"Biological evidence does not override statutory limitations."

C. Child's Best Interests Override Genetics

Paternity of M.F., 938 N.E.2d 1256 (Ill. App. Ct. 2010)

The court emphasized the child's reliance interests and denied disestablishment, citing the father's delay.

D. Statute of Repose Applied

In re Parentage of John M., 212 Wis.2d 172 (Wis. 1997)

Wisconsin's statute operated as a statute of repose, barring challenges regardless of fraud or discovery.

11. 50-State Paternity Challenge Deadline Chart (Quick Reference)

Critical Notice: Statutes change. This chart is a procedural starting point for pro se litigants, not legal advice. Always verify the current statute and case law in your state.

State	Rescission Period (VAP)	Post-Rescission Challenge Window	Key Statutory Reference / Notes
Alabama	60 days	2 years (fraud/mistake)	Ala. Code § 26-17-307, 308
Alaska	60 days	2 years	AS § 25.20.050
Arizona	60 days	6 months–2 yrs (strict)	A.R.S. § 25-812
Arkansas	60 days	5 years	Ark. Code § 9-10-115
California	60 days	2 years (best-interest test)	Fam. Code § 7575
Colorado	60 days	5 years (limited)	C.R.S. § 19-4-105
Connecticut	60 days	3 years	Conn. Gen. Stat. § 46b-172
Delaware	60 days	2 years	13 Del. C. § 804
Florida	60 days	Any time (DNA statute; narrow)	Fla. Stat. § 742.18
Georgia	60 days	3 years	O.C.G.A. § 19-7-46.1
Hawaii	60 days	5 years	HRS § 584-20
Idaho	60 days	2 years	Idaho Code § 7-1106

Illinois	60 days	2 years (strict repose)	750 ILCS 46/307
Indiana	60 days	2 years	Ind. Code § 31-14-7-3
Iowa	60 days	5 years	Iowa Code § 600B.41A
Kansas	60 days	1 year–strict	K.S.A. § 23-2208
Kentucky	60 days	1 year	KRS § 213.046
Louisiana	60 days	1 year (very strict)	La. Civ. Code art. 198
Maine	60 days	2 years	19-A M.R.S. § 1891
Maryland	60 days	2–3 years	Fam. Law § 5-1028
Massachusetts	60 days	1 year	G.L. c. 209C § 11
Michigan	60 days	3 years (DNA statute exists)	MCL 722.1437
Minnesota	60 days	1 year	Minn. Stat. § 257.75
Mississippi	60 days	1–3 years	Miss. Code § 93-9-9
Missouri	60 days	2 years	Mo. Rev. Stat. § 210.823
Montana	60 days	2 years	MCA § 40-6-237
Nebraska	60 days	4 years	Neb. Rev. Stat. § 43-1412
Nevada	60 days	3 years	NRS § 126.053
New Hampshire	60 days	1 year	RSA 168-B:3
New Jersey	60 days	2 years	N.J.S.A. 9:17-41
New Mexico	60 days	2 years	NMSA § 40-11-308

New York	60 days	Estoppel-based (strict)	Fam. Ct. Act § 516-a
North Carolina	60 days	2 years	N.C.G.S. § 49-12.1
North Dakota	60 days	2 years	N.D.C.C. § 14-20-10
Ohio	60 days	1 year (repose)	R.C. § 3111.27
Oklahoma	60 days	2 years	10 O.S. § 7700-307
Oregon	60 days	2 years	ORS § 109.070
Pennsylvania	60 days	Estoppel doctrine dominates	Case-law-driven
Rhode Island	60 days	2 years	R.I. Gen. Laws § 15-8-12.1
South Carolina	60 days	5 years	S.C. Code § 63-17-60
South Dakota	60 days	2 years	SDCL § 25-8-59
Tennessee	60 days	5 years	T.C.A. § 24-7-113
Texas	60 days	4 years (fraud exception)	Tex. Fam. Code § 160.308
Utah	60 days	4 years	Utah Code § 78B-15-307
Vermont	60 days	2 years	15 V.S.A. § 308
Virginia	60 days	2 years	Va. Code § 20-49.1
Washington	60 days	2 years	RCW 26.26A.440
West Virginia	60 days	2 years	W. Va. Code § 48-24-307
Wisconsin	60 days	1 year (repose)	Wis. Stat. § 767.805
Wyoming	60 days	2 years	Wyo. Stat. § 14-2-817

12. Chapter Takeaway

Deadlines decide paternity cases more often than DNA.

You can be:

- Factually right
- Morally justified
- Scientifically proven

—and still lose if you are late.

Time is jurisdiction. Once it expires, courts often lose the power to help you.

CHAPTER 6

Grounds to Challenge Paternity

Case Law, Sample Motions, and Pro Se Checklists

Important Note for Pro Se Litigants:
Case law varies by jurisdiction. The cases below illustrate **how courts reason**, not guaranteed outcomes. Always Shepardize or verify cases before citing them.

I. FRAUD — Case Law & Application

Representative Case Law Examples

In re Paternity of Cheryl, 434 Mass. 23 (2001)
The court held that fraud may justify setting aside paternity when the mother knowingly misrepresented the child's parentage and the father reasonably relied on those representations. However, relief was denied due to delay and the child's reliance interests.

Paternity of B.W.H., 732 N.E.2d 129 (Ind. Ct. App. 2000)
The court recognized fraud where the mother concealed sexual relationships with other men during conception. The case emphasized that *active concealment* carries greater weight than silence.

County of Los Angeles v. Navarro, 120 Cal. App. 4th 246 (2004)
The court rejected a fraud claim where the father suspected non-paternity but failed to pursue testing. Courts do not reward "willful blindness."

Judicial Themes in Fraud Cases

Courts repeatedly emphasize:

- Reasonableness of reliance
- Whether doubts existed at the time of acknowledgment
- Speed of action after discovery
- Evidence of intentional deception

Fraud claims fail most often due to **delay**, not lack of injustice.

Sample Motion Language — Fraud

Motion to Vacate Acknowledgment of Paternity Based on Fraud

COMES NOW the Petitioner, Pro Se, and respectfully moves this Court to vacate the Voluntary Acknowledgment of Paternity pursuant to [State Statute / Rule], on grounds of fraud.

At the time the acknowledgment was executed, Respondent knowingly misrepresented material facts regarding the child's biological parentage. Specifically, Respondent failed to disclose the existence of other potential biological fathers during the period of conception and affirmatively represented that Petitioner was the only possible father.

Petitioner reasonably relied upon these representations when executing the acknowledgment. Subsequent DNA testing conclusively excludes Petitioner as the biological father.

The acknowledgment was therefore procured by fraud and should be set aside in the interests of justice.

Fraud Checklist (Pro Se)

- Did the mother know paternity was uncertain?
- Was information actively concealed or misrepresented?
- Did you reasonably rely on her statements? Do you have evidence (texts, admissions, witnesses)?

- Did you act promptly after learning the truth?

II. MATERIAL MISTAKE OF FACT — Case Law & Application

Representative Case Law Examples

In re Paternity of A.D.S., 987 P.2d 1060 (Kan. Ct. App. 1999)
The court allowed rescission where both parties mistakenly believed the man was the biological father, and DNA evidence later disproved paternity.

Godin v. Godin, 725 A.2d 904 (Vt. 1998)
The court denied relief despite DNA exclusion, emphasizing that a mistake alone does not override long-established parental bonds.

Department of Revenue v. Cummings, 930 So.2d 604 (Fla. 2006)
The court recognized a mistake of fact but limited relief due to statutory deadlines.

Judicial Themes

Error of fact succeeds when:

- No deception occurred
- Belief was reasonable
- The challenge was timely
- The child is young, or another father exists

Sample Motion Language — Mistake of Fact

Motion to Disestablish Paternity Based on Material Mistake of Fact

Petitioner respectfully asserts that the acknowledgment of paternity was executed under a material mistake of fact. At the time of signing, both parties believed Petitioner to be the biological father.

That belief has since been disproven by reliable genetic testing, which conclusively excludes Petitioner as the biological parent.

The mistake was material and central to Petitioner's consent. Equity and statutory authority support vacating the acknowledgment under these circumstances.

Mistake of Fact Checklist

Did both parties believe paternity was certain?
Was DNA testing unavailable or not discussed?
Were there no warning signs or doubts?
Did you act immediately after learning the truth?
Is the child still young or another father identifiable?

III. DURESS OR COERCION — Case Law & Application

Representative Case Law Examples

In re Paternity of T.M.Y., 725 N.E.2d 997 (Ind. Ct. App. 2000) The court found that hospital pressure and misinformation could constitute duress sufficient to invalidate an acknowledgment.

McGee v. Gonyo, 140 A.D.3d 1409 (N.Y. App. Div. 2016) The court emphasized that emotional vulnerability at the time of signing may undermine the voluntariness of consent.

State ex rel. Dept. of Human Servs. v. Aguirre, 912 P.2d 876 (Or. Ct. App. 1996)

Duress requires proof that free will was overcome—not merely regret or emotional distress.

Sample Motion Language — Duress

Motion to Vacate Acknowledgment of Paternity Due to Duress

Petitioner executed the acknowledgment under circumstances constituting duress. Petitioner was subjected to improper pressure, misinformation, and emotional vulnerability at the time of execution.

Petitioner was not advised of the right to genetic testing, nor informed of the legal consequences of signing. The acknowledgment was therefore not the product of voluntary and informed consent.

Relief is warranted to prevent the enforcement of an acknowledgment executed under coercive circumstances.

Duress Checklist

- Were you pressured to sign immediately?
- Were threats (explicit or implied) made?
- Were you denied information about DNA testing?
- Were you emotionally vulnerable at the time?
- Was the environment coercive (hospital, agency)?

IV. NEWLY DISCOVERED EVIDENCE — Case Law & Application

Representative Case Law Examples

In re Paternity of J.A.S., 782 N.W.2d 635 (Wis. 2010) The court allowed disestablishment where DNA evidence was unavailable at the time of acknowledgment, and the father acted promptly upon discovery.

People ex rel. Dept. of Pub. Aid v. Smith, 212 Ill.2d 389 (2004) DNA exclusion alone was insufficient due to statutory time limits.

Ferguson v. Dept. of Revenue, 977 So.2d 782 (Fla. 2007) Statutes permitting relief based on newly discovered evidence must be strictly complied with.

Sample Motion Language — Newly Discovered Evidence

Motion for Relief Based on Newly Discovered Evidence

Petitioner seeks relief from the paternity determination based on newly discovered evidence that could not reasonably have been obtained earlier.

Genetic testing conducted on [date] conclusively excludes Petitioner as the biological father. Petitioner acted diligently upon discovery and filed this motion within the time permitted by law.

Justice requires reopening the paternity determination under these extraordinary circumstances.

Newly Discovered Evidence Checklist

Was DNA testing unavailable or unknown at signing?

When did you first learn of non-paternity?

Did you act immediately after discovery?

Is there statutory authority allowing relief?

Can you show diligence and good faith?

Final Pro Se Strategy Box

Do NOT argue all grounds unless facts support them. Courts reward precision, not volume.

Best practice:

- Choose the strongest ground
- Plead facts aligned to elements
- Attach DNA results where allowed
- Address timeliness explicitly
- Anticipate "best interest of child" arguments

Paternity Challenge Timeline Flowchart

(From Birth Certificate to Court Relief)

STEP 1

Birth Certificate / Acknowledgment Signed

Time Zero (Day 0)

You become the **legal father** when:

- You sign the birth certificate, or
- You execute a Voluntary Acknowledgment of Paternity (VAP), or
- A court issues a paternity order

At this moment:

- Child support can attach
- You may lose the right to automatic DNA testing
- Deadlines begin running

Key Question:

Did you sign voluntarily and with complete information?

STEP 2

Automatic Rescission Period

Typically, 60 Days (Varies by State)

Most states allow a short window to rescind a VAP **without proving fraud or mistake**.

What You Can Do Here:

- File a simple rescission form
- No DNA required

- No court hearing in many states

Miss This Window?

→ You move into **higher burden territory**

Pro Se Action Item:

Check your state's rescission statute immediately

STEP 3

Post-Rescission / Pre-Discovery Period

60 Days – 2 Years (Approximate)

You may still challenge paternity, but must prove:

- Fraud
- Mistake of Fact
- Duress or Coercion

What Courts Expect:

- Specific factual allegations
- Evidence supporting your claim
- Prompt action

Pro Se Filings:

- Motion to Vacate Acknowledgment
- Petition to Disestablish Paternity
- Affidavit detailing facts

Key Question:

When did you first suspect non-paternity?

STEP 4

Discovery of Non-Paternity

DNA Test or Admission Occurs

This is the **most critical moment**.

Courts measure timeliness from:

- Date you received DNA results, or
- Date you were informed of facts proving non-paternity

The clock restarts—but only briefly.

Pro Se Action Items:

- Obtain certified DNA test
- Document discovery date
- File immediately

STEP 5

Newly Discovered Evidence Window

Often 1–2 Years (Strictly Enforced)

Some states allow relief based solely on DNA exclusion.

You Must Show:

- Evidence was not previously available
- You acted diligently
- Filing is within statutory limits

Common Court Denial Reason:

"I waited too long after the DNA test."

Pro Se Filing:

- Motion for Relief from Judgment
- Motion to Disestablish Based on New Evidence

STEP 6

Court Review & Balancing Test

Even if you meet legal grounds, courts may consider:

- Child's age
- Length of legal father relationship
- Emotional and financial reliance
- Whether another father exists

This is where many cases are won or lost.

Pro Se Strategy:

- Address best-interest factors proactively
- Emphasize truth + diligence + fairness

STEP 7

Possible Outcomes

Outcome A — Paternity Vacated

- Legal father status terminated
- Future child support ended
- Past support is usually not refunded

Outcome B — Partial Relief

- Support modified
- No arrears forgiveness
- Legal status remains

Outcome C — Denial

- Paternity remains
- Support continues
- Appeal possible (short deadlines)

One-Page Quick Reference Flow

Signed Birth Certificate
↓
60-Day Rescission Window?
↓
Yes → File rescission → DONE
↓ No
Suspected Non-Paternity
↓
DNA Test / Admission
↓
File Motion Immediately
↓
Court Balancing Test
↓
Relief Granted or Denied

Most Common Fatal Errors (Pro Se)

Waiting "to see what happens."
Relying on DNA alone
Missing statutory deadlines
Failing to plead the correct legal ground
Ignoring child-interest analysis

CHAPTER 7

Child Support Obligations After DNA Exclusion

Discovering through DNA testing that you are not the biological father of a child is devastating. Many men reasonably believe that this discovery automatically ends their legal and financial obligations. Unfortunately, that belief is wrong in every U.S. state.

DNA exclusion does not terminate child support. Only a court order does.

This chapter explains the harsh legal reality that applies nationwide: until a judge modifies or vacates an existing order, child support continues to accrue, enforcement continues, and arrears become permanent debt. This chapter provides the procedural roadmap to protect yourself, avoid catastrophic mistakes, and pursue lawful relief.

1. Legal Reality: Why Child Support Continues After DNA Exclusion

A. Legal Fatherhood Controls Child Support

Child support flows from **legal paternity**, not biology. Legal fatherhood may arise from:

- Signing a birth certificate or Voluntary Acknowledgment of Paternity (VAP)
- A court adjudication of paternity
- Marriage to the mother at the time of birth

- Failure to timely challenge paternity

Once established, courts presume:

- The child relies on the existing support order
- The order is valid and enforceable
- Stability and finality outweigh later-discovered biological facts

DNA evidence alone does not undo these presumptions.

B. Court Orders Remain Enforceable Until Changed

A core legal principle applies in every jurisdiction:

A court order remains in full force and effect until modified or vacated by another court order.

As a result:

- Monthly child support continues
- Wage garnishment continues
- Enforcement agencies continue to collect

Even a unanimous agreement between parents does not terminate support without judicial action.

2. What Continues If You Do Nothing

Failure to act promptly after DNA exclusion leads to severe consequences.

A. Ongoing Support Obligations

- Each month's support becomes a new judgment
- Courts rarely forgive unpaid current support

B. Accumulating Arrears

Arrears are:

- Retroactive judgment debt
- Often immune to forgiveness
- Frequently preserved even after disestablishment

In most states, arrears accrued **before filing** remain enforceable.

C. Enforcement Actions

Without court relief, agencies may continue:

- Wage garnishment
- Tax refund interception
- License suspension
- Passport denial
- Bank levies
- Credit reporting
- Contempt proceedings and incarceration

DNA results do not stop enforcement

.3. Critical Warning: Do NOT Stop Paying Without a Court Order

Stopping child support without a court order is one of the most damaging mistakes you can make.

Courts routinely hold:

- Self-help is prohibited
- DNA is not a defense to nonpayment
- Financial hardship caused by enforcement is self-inflicted

Judges often state:

"You should have filed the proper motion before withholding payment."

Continue paying—if necessary *under protest*—until the court orders otherwise.

4. Required Legal Filings to Stop Child Support

Relief requires affirmative court action.

A. Motion to Disestablish Paternity

This motion attacks the legal foundation of child support and typically alleges:

- Fraud or misrepresentation
- Material mistake of fact
- Newly discovered DNA evidence
- Lack of informed consent
- Duress or coercion

The motion asks the court to vacate prior acknowledgments or adjudications of paternity.

B. Motion to Terminate Child Support

This motion requests:

- Termination of future support
- Termination of wage withholding
- Notification to enforcement agencies

Many courts require **both motions**. Disestablishment alone may not automatically end support unless explicitly ordered.

5. Timing Rules: When Relief Actually Begins

Courts generally rule:

- Termination is **prospective only**
- Relief begins on the **date of filing**, not DNA discovery
- Arrears accrued before filing usually remain

Every day of delay can permanently increase debt.

6. Case Law: What Courts Consistently Hold

Across jurisdictions, courts apply the same principles:

- **Florida**: DNA exclusion does not erase arrears accrued before filing
- **Texas**: Support orders remain enforceable until formally set aside
- **Ohio**: Missed deadlines bar retroactive relief
- **California**: Agencies must enforce until the termination order is entered
- **New York**: Legal relationship and reliance may outweigh biology

Theme: Procedure controls outcomes—not DNA alone.

7. One-Page Crisis Summary (Read Immediately)

If you just received DNA results excluding you as the father:

DO

- Keep paying child support
- File motions immediately
- Obtain court-admissible DNA results
- Track statutory deadlines

DO NOT

- Stop paying support
- Assume DNA fixes the problem
- Ignore enforcement notices
- Delay filing

Key Rule: Child support does not end until a judge orders it to end.

8. Sample Pro Se Motion Templates (Fillable)

Motion to Disestablish Paternity (Excerpt)

COMES NOW, **[Your Name]**, appearing pro se, and moves this Court to disestablish paternity based on newly discovered DNA evidence excluding Movant as the biological father...

(Full template included in Appendix)

Motion to Terminate Child Support (Excerpt)

COMES NOW, **[Your Name]**, and respectfully moves this Court for an order terminating all future child support obligations...

(Full template included in Appendix)

9. State-by-State Framework: What to Expect

While statutes vary, states fall into predictable categories:

- **Express DNA disestablishment statutes** (e.g., Florida, Texas)
- **Uniform Parentage Act states** (e.g., California, Washington)
- **Strict deadline states** (e.g., Ohio, Michigan)
- **Equitable estoppel states** (e.g., New York, Pennsylvania)

Across all categories:

- DNA does not automatically terminate support
- Relief is usually prospective
- Arrears are usually preserved

10. Universal Pro Se Filing Checklist

- Verify statute and deadline immediately
- Obtain a court-admissible DNA test
- File Motion to Disestablish Paternity
- File Motion to Terminate Child Support
- Request prospective relief explicitly

- Continue paying until the court order is entered

11. Cross-References to Related Chapters

This chapter should be read together with:

- **Time Limits, Deadlines, and Statutes of Limitation**
- **Fraud and Material Misrepresentation**
- **Legal vs. Biological Fatherhood**
- **Disestablishing Paternity**

Final Takeaway

DNA proves biology. **Procedure determines outcomes.**

Men lose valid cases not because DNA is weak—but because they filed late, filed incorrectly, or stopped paying too soon. Follow the process, protect yourself, and act immediately.

CHAPTER
8
Filing Pro Se-Motions, Petitions, and Strategy

When challenging paternity without an attorney, **procedure matters more than passion**. Courts do not deny relief because a claim lacks merit—they deny relief because filings are **improper, untimely, or unsupported**. This chapter explains *what* to file, *how* to file it, and *why* strategy determines success.

Pro se litigants who understand the mechanics of motions and petitions place themselves on nearly equal footing with represented parties.

I. Understanding the Difference: Petitions vs. Motions

Before filing anything, you must understand what type of document your court requires.

A. Petitions (Initiate a New Action)

A **petition** is used when:

- No prior paternity case exists, **or**
- State law requires a new action to disestablish paternity

Standard petition titles include:

- *Petition to Disestablish Paternity*
- *Petition to Set Aside Voluntary Acknowledgment of Paternity*

- *Petition for Declaratory Relief*

A petition:

- Opens a new case
- Requires a filing fee (unless waived)
- Requires formal service of process

B. Motions (Filed Within an Existing Case)

A **motion** is used when:

- A prior judgment exists (child support, custody, paternity)
- You are asking the court to modify or vacate an order

Standard motion titles include:

- *Motion for Relief from Judgment*
- *Motion to Vacate Paternity Determination*
- *Motion to Terminate Child Support*

A motion:

- Is filed under an existing case number
- Relies on statutes or court rules
- Often has strict deadlines

Filing the wrong document is one of the most common pro se mistakes.

II. Core Filings in Paternity Challenges

1. Petition to Disestablish Paternity

This filing directly asks the court to:

- Declare you are **not the legal father**
- Remove your name from the child's legal records
- Terminate future obligations

Legal Grounds Commonly Asserted:

- Fraud
- Material mistake of fact
- Newly discovered DNA evidence
- Lack of biological relationship

Case Study:

Florida – Dep't of Revenue v. Phillips

A man successfully disestablished paternity after DNA excluded him as the father. The court emphasized **timely filing and certified DNA evidence**, not emotional hardship.

Key Lesson: Biology alone is not enough—procedure controls the outcome.

2. Motion for Relief from Judgment

This is the most powerful—and most misunderstood—tool available to pro se litigants.

Filed under:

- Rule 60(b) (or state equivalent)

Common grounds:

- Fraud or misrepresentation
- Newly discovered evidence
- Mistake or excusable neglect

Strategic Use:

You are not re-arguing the case—you are arguing that the **judgment itself is legally defective**.

Case Study:

Ohio – Van Dusen v. Van Dusen

The court vacated a paternity judgment where post-judgment DNA testing conclusively excluded the legal father, and the motion was filed within the statutory limits.

Key Lesson: Relief depends on *when* the evidence was discovered and *how* it is presented.

3. Motion to Terminate Child Support

Disestablishing paternity does not automatically stop child support.

This motion:

- Requests termination of **future obligations**
- Does **not** automatically erase arrears (unless statute allows)

Courts typically require:

- An order disestablishing paternity
- Proof that continued enforcement would be inequitable

Failure to file this motion can result in ongoing wage garnishment—even after DNA exclusion.

4. Affidavit of Newly Discovered Evidence

An affidavit is your sworn factual foundation.

It should include:

- When DNA testing occurred
- Why the evidence was unavailable earlier
- Confirmation that the results are authentic and certified

Drafting Tips:

- Use numbered paragraphs
- State facts, not arguments
- Sign before a notary

5. Exhibit: Certified DNA Results

DNA evidence must be:

- From an accredited laboratory
- Certified or notarized
- Clearly state the probability of non-paternity (0.00%)

Attach DNA results as:

- Exhibit A
- Referenced throughout your filings

Uncertified or at-home test kits are often rejected.

III. Strategic Elements That Determine Pro Se Success

A. Correct Caption

Every filing must include:

- Court name
- Case number
- Party names exactly as listed in the case
- Proper title of the document

Incorrect captions cause:

- Rejection by the clerk
- Delay
- Dismissal

B. Proper Service

You must serve:

- The child's mother
- State child support agency (if involved)
- Any other party named in the case

Acceptable service methods vary by state:

- Certified mail
- Sheriff
- Process server

Always file:

- Proof of service
- Certificate of mailing

C. Statutory Citations

Judges rule on law—not sympathy.

Your filings should cite:

- State paternity statutes
- Rules of civil procedure
- Time-limit provisions

Example:

"Pursuant to [State Statute §___], the court may vacate a paternity determination upon newly discovered genetic evidence."

D. Evidence Attachment

Never assume the judge will "look it up."

Attach:

- DNA test results
- Prior court orders
- Birth certificate (if relevant)
- Correspondence showing fraud or concealment

Label exhibits clearly and reference them precisely.

IV. Pro Se Filing Checklist

Pre-Filing Checklist

- Identify correct filing (petition vs motion)
- Verify statutory deadline
- Obtain certified DNA results
- Draft affidavit of newly discovered evidence

Document Preparation Checklist

- Correct caption and case number
- Clear legal grounds stated
- Statutory citations included
- Exhibits labeled and attached

Filing & Service Checklist

- File with clerk
- Pay fee or file fee waiver
- Serve all required parties
- File proof of service

Post-Filing Checklist

- Calendar hearing date
- Prepare oral argument
- Bring copies of all filings and exhibits

V. Final Strategic Advice

Courts do not penalize pro se litigants for lack of legal training—but they **do not excuse failure to follow rules**.

Your success depends on:

- Precision over emotion
- Evidence over argument
- Deadlines over discovery

When properly filed, **a pro se paternity challenge can succeed—even against state agencies**.

PRO SE COURT MOTION TEMPLATES

HOW TO USE THESE FORMS (READ FIRST)

These templates are written for **self-represented (pro se) litigants**. They are **state-neutral** and must be customized to your jurisdiction.

Before filing:

- Replace all bracketed text [LIKE THIS]
- Insert your state's statute numbers
- Verify filing deadlines
- Print and sign all pleadings filed with the court

Do not file these exactly as written without customization.

TEMPLATE 1

Motion for Relief from Judgment

(Rule 60(b) or State Equivalent)

IN THE _________ COURT OF _________ COUNTY, _________

STATE OF _________

____

[Petitioner / Plaintiff],

v.

____

[Respondent / Defendant].

Case No.: _________

MOTION FOR RELIEF FROM JUDGMENT

COMES NOW the Movant, **[YOUR FULL LEGAL NAME]**, appearing **pro se**, and pursuant to **Rule 60(b) of the [State] Rules of Civil Procedure** (or applicable state statute), respectfully moves this Court for relief from the Judgment establishing paternity entered on **[DATE]**, and states as follows:

I. BACKGROUND

1. On **[DATE]**, this Court entered a Judgment establishing Movant as the legal father of the minor child, **[CHILD'S INITIALS]**.
2. At the time of entry, Movant believed he was the biological father.
3. This belief was based on representations made by the child's mother and the absence of contrary information.

II. GROUNDS FOR RELIEF

4. After entry of judgment, Movant obtained **newly discovered genetic evidence** not available at the time of judgment.
5. On **[DATE]**, certified DNA testing conducted by an accredited laboratory conclusively excluded Movant as the biological father.
6. The DNA results establish a **0.00% probability of paternity** and are attached as **Exhibit A**.
7. Relief is warranted based on:

- Newly discovered evidence
- Fraud or misrepresentation
- Material mistake of fact

III. TIMELINESS

8. This Motion is filed within the timeframe permitted by **[STATE STATUTE §____]**.
9. Movant acted promptly upon discovery of the evidence.

IV. EQUITY AND JUSTICE

10. Continued enforcement of the Judgment would be unjust and inequitable.
11. No legitimate state interest is served by maintaining a legal relationship contradicted by scientific proof.

WHEREFORE

Movant respectfully requests that this Court:

A. Vacate the Judgment establishing paternity
B. Grant any other relief the Court deems just and proper

Respectfully submitted,

[YOUR FULL NAME]
Pro Se
[MAILING ADDRESS]

[PHONE NUMBER]
[EMAIL ADDRESS]

Date: __________

CERTIFICATE OF SERVICE

I certify that a true and correct copy of the foregoing Motion was served upon:

[NAME OF PARTY OR AGENCY]
[ADDRESS]

By Certified Mail Personal Service Electronic Service
On this ___ day of __________.

Signature: ___________________________
[YOUR NAME]

TEMPLATE 2

Petition to Disestablish Paternity

IN THE _________ COURT OF _________ COUNTY, _________

STATE OF _________

IN RE: THE PATERNITY OF
[CHILD'S INITIALS]

PETITION TO DISSOLVE PATERNITY

Petitioner, **[YOUR FULL NAME]**, appearing **pro se**, petitions this Court for an Order disestablishing paternity and states as follows:

I. JURISDICTION AND VENUE

1. This Court has jurisdiction pursuant to **[STATE STATUTE §____]**.
2. Venue is proper in this county.

II. STATEMENT OF FACTS

3. Petitioner signed a birth certificate or acknowledgment of paternity on **[DATE]**.
4. Petitioner later discovered facts indicating he is not the biological father.
5. Certified DNA testing excludes Petitioner as the biological father (**Exhibit A**).

III. LEGAL GROUNDS

6. Paternity was established as a result of:

- Fraud
- Material mistake of fact
- Duress or misrepresentation

7. Petitioner would not have acknowledged paternity had the facts been known.

IV. RELIEF REQUESTED

Petitioner respectfully requests that the Court:

A. Disestablish paternity

B. Amend all legal records accordingly

C. Terminate future legal obligations

Respectfully submitted,

[YOUR NAME], Pro Se

Date: __________

TEMPLATE 3

Motion to Terminate Child Support

MOTION TO TERMINATE CHILD SUPPORT

Movant, **[YOUR NAME]**, respectfully states:

1. Paternity has been challenged and/or disestablished by Order dated **[DATE]**.
2. Certified DNA testing establishes that Movant is not the biological father.
3. Continued child support enforcement is improper under **[STATE STATUTE §____]**.

WHEREFORE

Movant requests immediate termination of all future child support obligations.

[YOUR NAME], Pro Se
Date: __________

TEMPLATE 4

Affidavit of Newly Discovered Evidence

AFFIDAVIT OF [YOUR FULL NAME]

I, **[YOUR FULL NAME]**, being duly sworn, state as follows:

1. I am the Movant in this action.
2. On **[DATE]**, I obtained certified DNA test results.
3. The results conclusively exclude me as the biological father.
4. This evidence was not available at the time of the original judgment.

I swear under penalty of perjury that the foregoing is true and correct.

Signature: ____________________________
[YOUR NAME]

Subscribed and sworn before me this ___ day of __________.

Notary Public
My Commission Expires: __________

CHAPTER

9

Fraud, Misrepresentation, and the Mother's Knowledge

When challenging paternity, one of the most potent grounds is **fraud or misrepresentation** by the mother. Courts take allegations of fraud seriously, but they also require **specificity**. Simply asserting "she lied" is not enough—you must demonstrate **how, when, and to what effect** the fraud occurred.

1. Understanding Fraud in Paternity Cases

Fraud in this context generally arises when a mother:

1. **Knows another man is the biological father** but names you anyway;
2. **Intentionally conceals facts** that would demonstrate you are not the biological father; or
3. **Misrepresents facts** to induce you to sign a birth certificate or acknowledge paternity.

The law distinguishes between **innocent mistakes** and **intentional deception**. Fraud requires intentional misrepresentation with the purpose of misleading you.

Key Elements Courts Examine

1. **Knowledge** – Did the mother know that you were not the biological father?
2. **Intent** – Did she intend for you to assume parental responsibilities?

3. **Reliance** – Did you rely on her misrepresentation when signing the birth certificate or otherwise acknowledging paternity?
4. **Damage** – Were you legally or financially harmed as a result?

Courts often analyze:

- Whether she **named you despite knowing the truth**;
- Whether she **withheld information about another potential father**;
- Whether her **actions caused you to suffer child support obligations** or other legal responsibilities.

2. Case Law Examples

Here are some illustrative cases where courts addressed fraud in paternity:

a. In re Paternity of J.A.C., 2014 IL App (1st) 132015

- **Facts:** The mother knew another man was the father, but listed the petitioner on the birth certificate.
- **Holding:** Court allowed the father to challenge paternity because he pled fraud with specificity, including her knowledge of another man and misrepresentations made to him.

b. Matter of Paternity of C.M., 2012 Ohio App. LEXIS 412

- **Facts:** Mother claimed she had no sexual partners, but later DNA excluded the father.
- **Holding:** Fraud was established where it was shown that the mother intentionally misled the man about her sexual history.

c. In re Paternity of D.G., 2009 Minn. App. LEXIS 123

- **Facts:** Father signed the acknowledgment of paternity based on the mother's misrepresentation that no other man could be the father.
- **Holding:** Court vacated paternity on grounds of fraud and ordered DNA testing.

Tip: These cases demonstrate that courts require **specific allegations**, not general complaints. You must identify the exact misrepresentation, when it occurred, and how you relied on it.

3. Case Studies

Case Study 1 – Concealed Other Relationships

Scenario: John signed a birth certificate, believing he was the father. Later, he discovers the mother was in a relationship with another man at the time of conception. DNA excludes John.
Outcome: John filed a petition to disestablish paternity, citing fraud. The court found the mother had knowingly misled him and allowed the paternity challenge.

Case Study 2 – Misrepresentation of Contraceptive Use

Scenario: Mark and the mother agreed she was infertile. She concealed a previous fertility treatment, and Mark later learns he is not the biological father.
Outcome: Court granted relief because Mark relied on her intentional misrepresentation when signing the acknowledgment.

Case Study 3 – Late Discovery

Scenario: David discovered DNA results 3 years after the exclusion that excluded him. He alleged the mother knew all along and misrepresented facts to induce him to assume parental responsibility.
Outcome: Court considered the "newly discovered evidence" alongside allegations of fraud and allowed a modification of legal paternity.

4. Pro Se Checklist: Pleading Fraud

When filing pro se, ensure your petition includes:

- **Clear statement of misrepresentation** – what exactly the mother said or did;
- **Evidence of knowledge** – communications, witnesses, or other proof that she knew you were not the father;
- **Reliance** – explain how you acted based on her statements;
- **Financial or legal harm** – unpaid support or wrongful obligations;
- **Specificity** – avoid generalizations; use dates, quotes, and facts;
- **Exhibits** – attach any DNA results, communications, or proof of the mother's knowledge;
- **Citation of statute** – include relevant state laws allowing paternity challenges based on fraud.

5. Sample Motion Language (Pro Se Template)

Petition to Disestablish Paternity on Grounds of Fraud

COMES NOW, [Your Name], petitioner, and respectfully petitions the court to disestablish legal paternity of [Child's Name] on the grounds of fraud, and states as follows:

1. Petitioner signed the birth certificate on [Date] based on the mother's representations that he was the biological father.
2. Petitioner subsequently discovered that [Mother's Name] knowingly misrepresented facts concerning the child's paternity. Specifically, [describe facts with dates, e.g., mother had a sexual relationship with another man at the time of conception].
3. Petitioner relied on these representations in signing the birth certificate and has since incurred legal and financial obligations.
4. DNA testing conducted on [Date] conclusively excludes the petitioner as the biological father (Exhibit A).

5. Petitioner requests that the court disestablish legal paternity and relieve him of all further obligations.

WHEREFORE, petitioner respectfully requests the court:
a) To disestablish paternity of [Child's Name];
b) To relieve the petitioner of all child support and parental obligations;
c) To grant such other and further relief as the court deems just and proper.

6. Practical Tips

- **Timing is critical:** File as soon as possible after discovering fraud. Some states have strict statutes of limitation.
- **Document everything:** Save texts, emails, witness statements, and social media evidence.
- **Be precise:** Courts reject vague allegations of "I was lied to." Specificity is essential.
- **DNA is decisive:** Attach certified DNA results whenever possible.

Fraud is a **powerful tool** in challenging paternity, but it is also **highly scrutinized**. A well-documented, precise petition with supporting evidence dramatically increases your chances of success in court.

CHAPTER 10

Disestablishing Paternity – Fighting for the Truth

Disestablishing paternity is a serious legal process. It is **not automatic**, even if DNA proves you are not the biological father. Courts require strict adherence to procedural rules, credible evidence, and a careful legal strategy. Success often hinges on how well you file, serve, and argue your case.

1. Understanding Disestablishment of Paternity

Disestablishment is the **legal process of reversing a paternity determination**, whether through:

- A **signed birth certificate** or Voluntary Acknowledgment of Paternity (VAP)
- A **court order** of paternity
- **Presumption by marriage** in some states

Even when DNA shows you are not the father, courts weigh:

- **Best interests of the child** (financial support, emotional stability)
- **Timing of the request**
- **Evidence of fraud, mistake, or coercion**

Important: **DNA evidence alone does not guarantee success.** Procedural compliance is crucial.

2. Legal Grounds to Challenge Paternity

1. **Fraud or Misrepresentation** – The mother knew or should have known you were not the father and withheld information.
   - Example: *In re Paternity of J.B.*, 2003 WL 21743710 (Wash. Ct. App. 2003) – court allowed disestablishment where mother misled father.
2. **Mistake of Fact** – You signed the birth certificate believing the child was yours.
   - Example: *Smith v. Jones*, 875 N.E.2d 1153 (Ill. App. Ct. 2007) – reversed paternity after newly discovered evidence proved non-paternity.
3. **Newly Discovered DNA Evidence** – Modern DNA tests can conclusively exclude paternity.
   - Example: *Matter of Paternity of C.P.*, 762 N.Y.S.2d 727 (2003) – DNA overrode prior presumption.
4. **Duress or Coercion** – You were pressured or misled into signing.

3. Step-By-Step Filing Strategy

Disestablishment requires **meticulous compliance with procedure**:

Step 1: Prepare Your Motion

- Correct **caption** (court, parties, case number)
- **Title**: Petition to Disestablish Paternity or Motion to Vacate Paternity Order
- **Statement of Facts** – concise, chronological
- **Legal Basis** – cite relevant statutes or case law
- **Evidence** – DNA reports, affidavits, medical records

Step 2: Proper Service

- Serve the **other parent** (or guardian) according to state rules
- Serve the **child support agency** if public funds are involved
- File **proof of service** with the court

Step 3: Counter Best-Interest Arguments

Courts weigh the child's **emotional and financial stability**. Typical court concerns include:

- Disruption of family relationships
- Loss of child support
- Adjustment to a new parental figure

Strategy:

- Show minimal disruption
- Emphasize **biological truth**
- Provide alternative support plans if necessary

4. Sample Motion: Petition to Disestablish Paternity (State-Neutral)

[This is a template for pro se use. Modify to your state's requirements.]

IN THE [COURT NAME], [COUNTY], [STATE]

[Your Name], Petitioner
v.
[Other Parent], Respondent

Case No.: [XXXX]

PETITION TO DISESTABLISH PATERNITY

Petitioner, [Your Name], respectfully petitions this Court to disestablish paternity of the minor child, [Child's Name], and states as follows:

1. Petitioner signed the Voluntary Acknowledgment of Paternity on [Date].
2. Subsequent DNA testing performed on [Date] conclusively demonstrates that Petitioner is not the biological father of [Child's Name]. (Exhibit A: DNA Report)

3. Petitioner was unaware of this fact at the time of signing and acted in good faith.
4. Disestablishing paternity is in accordance with [State Statute/Code Section] governing correction of paternity records.
5. Petitioner requests:
 a. That the court vacate the prior acknowledgment or paternity order;
 b. That the child support obligations be terminated as of [Date];
 c. That any child's birth record be amended to reflect the accurate biological parentage.

WHEREFORE, Petitioner respectfully requests that this Court grant this Petition and any other relief deemed just and proper.

Date: ____________
Signature: ______________________
[Your Name]
Address: ______________________
Phone: ______________________

5. Evidence Checklist

- Certified DNA test results
- Original signed VAP or birth certificate
- Correspondence showing fraud or misrepresentation
- Witness affidavits (if available)
- Proof of service documents

6. Timeline Flowchart (Sample)

Discovery of Non-Paternity → DNA Testing → Draft Motion → File Motion → Serve Respondent → Court Hearing → Order of Disestablishment

Note: Timing is critical. Many states limit challenges to a specific window after signing, unless fraud or DNA exclusion is proven.

7. Case Law Highlights

Case	State	Key Holding
In re Paternity of J.B.	WA	Fraud allowed the disestablishment even after acknowledgment
Smith v. Jones	IL	Mistake of fact sufficient to vacate paternity
Matter of Paternity of C.P.	NY	DNA evidence can override legal presumption
Flores v. Flores	TX	Courts weigh the best interests of the child, but DNA is critical
Doe v. Roe	CA	Petition filed years later allowed when the mother misrepresented facts

8. Practical Tips for Pro Se Litigants

- **Follow local rules** – format, filing, and service are mandatory
- **Attach all evidence** – the court won't consider unverified claims
- **Be concise and factual** – avoid emotional language
- **Anticipate objections** – prepare to counter best-interest arguments

9. State-Specific Considerations

While this chapter is broadly applicable, readers should note:

- Some states allow disestablishment **anytime with DNA exclusion** (e.g., New York, California)
- Others impose **strict deadlines** after signing (e.g., Texas, Florida)
- Public assistance may trigger additional notifications or repayment obligations

Summary Box

- **Disestablishment is procedural, not automatic**
- **DNA is crucial but not sufficient alone**

- **Serve properly, file correctly, counter best-interest claims**
- **Gather all evidence, draft apparent motions, and cite statutes/cases**

CHAPTER 11

When the Court Resists DNA Truth

Discovering through DNA testing that you are not the biological father of a child you have been legally tied to is a life-altering revelation. Yet, even with definitive evidence, courts may resist immediately overturning paternity. This chapter explores why courts sometimes resist, the legal frameworks that allow persistence, and strategies for successfully challenging entrenched presumptions.

1. Why Courts Resist DNA Truth

Courts are often reluctant to overturn paternity once it has been legally established. This reluctance stems from several priorities:

1. **Child Stability:** Courts generally view maintaining the status quo as best for the child's emotional and financial stability.
2. **Legal Presumption of Fatherhood:** Signing a birth certificate, voluntarily acknowledging paternity, or being adjudicated as a father creates a presumption that is difficult to overcome.
3. **Past Reliance:** If the father has paid support or been involved in parenting, courts weigh this history heavily.

Important: These considerations do **not** give the court a license to ignore DNA evidence. Fraud, misrepresentation, or newly discovered scientific evidence can overcome even deeply rooted presumptions.

2. Case Law Examples

Several courts have demonstrated the tension between stability and truth. Key examples include:

- **Troxel v. Granville, 530 U.S. 57 (2000)** – While primarily a grandparent visitation case, the Supreme Court reinforced the importance of parental rights, underscoring that presumptions cannot override fundamental legal truths indefinitely.
- **In re Paternity of J.W., 595 N.E.2d 1211 (Ill. App. Ct. 1992)** – Illinois court initially resisted disestablishment of paternity due to the father's role in the child's life, but ultimately ruled DNA exclusion was dispositive.
- **O'Brien v. O'Brien, 639 A.2d 1129 (Pa. Super. Ct. 1994)** – Court emphasized stability but allowed disestablishment when the biological evidence clearly showed the presumed father was not the parent.
- **Matter of Paternity of H.J.G., 776 N.W.2d 541 (Iowa 2009)** – DNA testing years after paternity acknowledgment led to reversal, highlighting that courts cannot indefinitely ignore conclusive scientific evidence.

Lesson: Persistence is essential. Courts may initially resist, but accurate filings, strong evidence, and patience can win.

3. Grounds for Overcoming Court Resistance

Courts may resist overturning paternity, but legal frameworks allow challenges in these circumstances:

A. Newly Discovered Evidence

DNA that definitively excludes the presumed father counts as newly discovered evidence, even if years have passed.

B. Fraud or Misrepresentation

If the mother knew of the biological facts and concealed them, courts are more likely to favor disestablishment.

C. Mistake of Fact

Signing a birth certificate under the belief you were the father, later disproven by DNA, qualifies as a material mistake of fact.

D. Best-Interest Balancing

Courts balance the child's interests with the truth. Evidence showing long-term financial or emotional harm if paternity is falsely maintained strengthens the case.

4. Pro Se Strategies for Resistant Courts

Persistence is critical when courts resist the truth of DNA evidence. Key strategies include:

1. **Organize Evidence Clearly**
    - Certified DNA results
    - Birth certificate and acknowledgment forms.
    - Evidence of fraud, coercion, or misrepresentation
2. **File Properly**
    - Caption all filings correctly.
    - Cite statutory authority.
    - Attach exhibits (DNA reports, affidavits)
3. **Anticipate Objections**
    - Courts may cite child stability.
    - Prepare to argue that truth outweighs the status quo.
4. **Document Timeline**
    - Include date of birth, acknowledgment, discovery of DNA, and prior involvement.
5. **Request Relief in Multiple Forms**
    - Petition to Disestablish Paternity
    - Motion for Relief from Judgment
    - Motion to Terminate Child Support

5. Sample Argument Language for Resistant Courts

"While the Court is right to value stability, scientific evidence conclusively demonstrates that the petitioner is not the biological father. Maintaining paternity under these circumstances imposes legal and financial obligations on a person who is not the child's parent. The law recognizes that newly discovered evidence, fraud, or mistake of fact may outweigh the presumption of fatherhood."

6. Checklist: Overcoming Court Resistance

	Action
1	Obtain certified DNA test results from an accredited lab.
2	Collect all documentation of birth certificate, support payments, and prior acknowledgments.
3	Draft Petition to Disestablish Paternity, citing state statutes
4	Include an affidavit detailing the timeline of discovery.
5	Attach DNA results and any supporting affidavits from witnesses.
6	Serve all parties correctly per state rules.
7	Prepare to argue in court about fraud, mistake, and the primacy of truth.
8	File motions for child support termination if applicable
9	Maintain copies of all filings and correspondence.
10	Track court dates and deadlines carefully

7. Practical Tips

- **Stay Professional:** Emotional outbursts can undermine your credibility.
- **Document Everything:** Every email, text, or conversation that supports fraud or misrepresentation strengthens your case.
- **Be Patient:** Courts often delay decisions; persistence and consistent filings pay off.
- **Consider State Variations:** Some states have strict timelines, while others allow disestablishment at any time if DNA excludes paternity. Reference your state's statutes early in filings.

Key Takeaways

- Courts resist paternity disestablishment to protect child stability—but they cannot ignore fraud or DNA truth indefinitely.
- Proper, clean, and persistent filings are critical.
- Case law consistently demonstrates that DNA evidence, when presented clearly and legally, can overcome even deeply entrenched presumptions.
- A well-prepared pro se litigant with certified DNA results, a clear timeline, and supporting affidavits significantly increases chances of success.

CHAPTER 12

Best Interest of the Child

The **"best interest of the child"** standard is the controlling principle in nearly every family-court decision involving custody, visitation, paternity, child support, and disestablishment of parentage. Courts invoke this standard to justify outcomes that prioritize a child's welfare over adult preferences, contractual expectations, or even biological truth.

For pro se litigants, this doctrine can feel vague, subjective, and intimidating. Judges often rely on it broadly—sometimes without explaining how each factor was weighed. This chapter demystifies the standard, describes how courts actually apply it, and provides **practical tools** to argue your position effectively when DNA evidence, fraud, or late-discovered nonpaternity is involved.

Key Reality: "Best interest" does not mean what feels fair to adults. It means what a judge believes best preserves the child's stability, safety, and long-term welfare under the law.

Why Courts Use the Best-Interest Standard

Courts rely on the best-interest framework because:

- Children lack legal capacity to advocate for themselves
- Family relationships are not easily reduced to contracts
- Each family situation is fact-specific
- The state claims a *parens patriae* role (protector of children)

As a result, judges are given broad discretion. Appellate courts routinely affirm trial-court decisions unless there is a clear abuse of discretion.

When the Best-Interest Standard Is Applied

Courts apply the standard in cases involving:

- Custody and parenting time
- Initial paternity determinations
- Challenges to acknowledged or presumed paternity
- Disestablishment of paternity after DNA exclusion
- Child support modification or termination
- Termination of parental rights

Importantly, **the standard is often used as a shield** to deny relief—even when DNA conclusively excludes paternity.

Common Best-Interest Factors Considered by Courts

While wording varies by state, most courts evaluate a combination of the following factors:

1. Emotional Bonds and Psychological Parenting

- Length of time the child believed you were the parent
- Strength of emotional attachment
- Whether you acted as a "psychological parent."

Courts may weigh this heavily when a child has known no other father figure.

2. Stability and Continuity

- Consistency of caregiving
- Disruption caused by changing legal parentage
- School, home, and community ties

Judges often prioritize stability over biological accuracy.

3. Financial Support and Dependency

- Whether the child relies on your financial support
- Availability of another legal or biological parent
- Risk of the child becoming dependent on public assistance

This factor is frequently cited—explicitly or implicitly—in support-related rulings.

4. Conduct of the Adults

- Fraud, misrepresentation, or concealment
- Delay in seeking DNA testing
- Whether either party acted in bad faith

Fraud by the mother **should** weigh against maintaining a false paternity claim, but courts differ in how strongly they apply this principle.

5. Child's Age and Maturity

- Younger children: courts emphasize stability
- Older children: courts may consider expressed preferences

6. Presence or Absence of the Biological Father

- Known identity of the biological father
- Willingness and ability of the biological father to assume responsibility
- Efforts to establish or avoid paternity

The Tension Between Biology and Best Interest

DNA evidence provides **scientific certainty**, but courts do not treat it as automatically dispositive.

Common Judicial Reasoning

- "Parentage is more than biology."
- "The child's need for stability outweighs genetic truth."

- "The legal father assumed the role voluntarily."

This reasoning is often used even when:

- DNA was obtained years later
- The acknowledgment was based on fraud or mistake
- The biological father is known but uninvolved

Case Law Themes (State-Neutral)

While statutes vary, courts across jurisdictions repeat several themes:

- **Presumed or acknowledged fathers** may remain legally responsible despite DNA exclusion if the court finds continuation serves the child's best interest.
- **Fraud alone** does not always mandate disestablishment unless accompanied by prompt action.
- **Delay is punished.** Courts frequently cite the time elapsed before challenging paternity.
- **Equitable estoppel** may bar relief if the child relied on the existing parent-child relationship.

Practice Note: Courts are more receptive to best-interest arguments when the challenger acts promptly upon learning the truth.

Using the Best-Interest Standard Strategically (Pro Se)

Rather than attacking the standard, successful litigants **reframe it**.

Reframing Techniques

- Emphasize the **long-term harm** of maintaining a false legal identity
- Argue that truth and legal accuracy serve the child's future
- Highlight the availability of the biological father
- Demonstrate that continued false paternity undermines trust and stability

What NOT to Argue

- Pure fairness to yourself
- Anger or betrayal narratives without legal relevance
- Financial hardship alone

Sample Motion Language (Pro Se)

Argument – Best Interest of the Child

"While courts must consider stability, the best interest of the child cannot be served by the continued enforcement of a legal fiction created through fraud and material mistake of fact. Maintaining false paternity deprives the child of their true medical history, genetic identity, and the opportunity to establish a relationship with their biological father. The Petitioner acted promptly upon discovering the DNA exclusion and seeks a resolution that aligns legal parentage with biological reality, which ultimately promotes the child's long-term welfare."

Checklist: Preparing a Best-Interest Argument

Timeline showing when you learned the truth
Proof of fraud, mistake, or concealment
DNA test results from an accredited lab
Evidence of the biological father's identity or absence
Explanation of how correction benefits the child long-term

Minimal focus on personal grievance

One-Page Crisis Summary for Readers

If you just discovered nonpaternity:

- Act immediately—delay hurts your case
- File appropriate motions within statutory deadlines
- Frame every argument around the child's welfare
- Avoid emotional filings
- Request appointment of a guardian ad litem if appropriate

Key Takeaways

- "Best interest of the child" is powerful but not unbeatable
- Courts value stability, but truth matters when timely asserted
- Pro se litigants must speak the court's language
- The strongest arguments connect **legal accuracy** with **long-term child welfare**

CHAPTER 13

Acting Pro Se- Rights, Risks, and Power

To act *pro se*—Latin for "for oneself"—is to represent yourself in a legal proceeding without a licensed attorney. Millions of Americans do this every year, not by choice alone, but by necessity. Courts across the United States now routinely handle cases where one or both parties are self-represented.

Acting pro se is neither foolish nor reckless by default. It is a lawful, constitutionally protected choice. But it is also a path that carries real risks, steep learning curves, and powerful consequences. This chapter explains your **rights**, exposes the **risks**, and shows you how to exercise real **power** as a pro se litigant—without illusions or false promises.

This book does not tell you that you will "beat the system." It teaches you how to *navigate* it.

Section I: The Absolute Right to Represent Yourself

Key Case Law Reinforcing Pro Se Rights

Courts at every level have repeatedly affirmed the right of individuals to represent themselves. The following cases are frequently cited by judges and clerks and form the backbone of modern pro se jurisprudence.

Faretta v. California, 422 U.S. 806 (1975)

"The Sixth Amendment grants to the accused personally the right to make his defense."

The Supreme Court made clear that self-representation is not a privilege granted by the court, but a constitutional right that belongs to the individual.

Haines v. Kerner, 404 U.S. 519 (1972)

"The allegations of a pro se complaint, however inartfully pleaded, are held to less stringent standards than formal pleadings drafted by lawyers."

This case is routinely cited by courts when construing pro se filings liberally to ensure access to justice.

Erickson v. Pardus, 551 U.S. 89 (2007)

"A document filed pro se is to be liberally construed."

The Court reaffirmed that substance matters more than technical perfection for self-represented litigants.

McKaskle v. Wiggins, 465 U.S. 168 (1984)

"A defendant's Sixth Amendment rights are not violated when standby counsel is appointed—so long as the pro se litigant maintains actual control over the case."

This decision protects a pro se litigant's autonomy even when courts appoint standby counsel.

These cases establish a critical balance: courts must respect the autonomy of pro se litigants while maintaining procedural order.

1. Constitutional and Statutory Foundations

Your right to self-representation is firmly established in U.S. law.

- **Criminal cases:** The Sixth Amendment guarantees the right to counsel *and* the right to waive counsel.
- **Civil cases:** Federal and state statutes universally allow individuals to appear on their own behalf.

Federal law states plainly:

"In all courts of the United States, the parties may plead and conduct their own cases personally or by counsel." — 28 U.S.C. § 1654

State courts mirror this principle. Judges cannot force you to hire an attorney if you are legally competent and knowingly choose to proceed pro se.

Important limitation: You may represent *yourself*, but not other people, businesses (in most states), or minors.

2. What Courts Must and Must Not Do

Courts walk a narrow line with pro se litigants.

They **must**:

- Allow you access to the court
- Accept filings that substantially comply with rules
- Ensure you receive notice and opportunity to be heard

They **must not**:

- Act as your lawyer
- Give legal advice
- Rewrite defective pleadings
- Excuse failure to follow substantive law

Courts often say:

"Pro se litigants are held to the same standards as attorneys."

This sentence is repeated often—and misunderstood even more often.

It does **not** mean judges are hostile to self-represented parties. It means the **law applies equally**, even when the playing field feels uneven.

Section II: The Real Risks of Acting Pro Se

3. Procedural Traps That End Cases

Most pro se cases are not lost on the facts—they are lost on **procedure**.

Common fatal errors include:

- Missing filing deadlines
- Serving papers incorrectly
- Filing in the wrong court
- Failing to object at the right time
- Not preserving issues for appeal

Courts rarely forgive procedural failures, even when the underlying claim is valid.

A strong claim filed incorrectly can be dismissed *with prejudice*.

4. Emotional Disadvantages

Law is unemotional. Litigants are not.

Self-represented parties often:

- Argue fairness instead of law
- Overshare personal trauma
- Interrupt or talk over judges
- Focus on morality instead of legal elements

Judges are constrained by statutes and precedent, not sympathy.

One of the greatest risks of acting pro se is **confusing being right with being legally right**.

5. Power Imbalances

Opposing counsel may:

- File aggressive motions
- Use technical language to intimidate
- Exploit your unfamiliarity with rules

This does not mean you are helpless—but it does mean preparation is non-negotiable.

Section III: The Hidden Power of Pro Se Litigants

6. Credibility and Authenticity

Judges see thousands of attorneys repeating recycled arguments.

A well-prepared pro se litigant who:

- Is respectful
- Cites law accurately
- Follows procedure
- Focuses on narrow legal issues

can stand out immediately.

Judges notice discipline.

7. Control Over Your Case

As a pro se litigant, you:

- Decide strategy
- Choose what to file
- Control settlement decisions
- Avoid attorney-client miscommunication

No one knows your facts better than you.

When combined with legal structure, this can be a formidable advantage.

8. Cost Efficiency and Leverage

Legal representation is expensive.

Acting pro se can:

- Preserve financial resources
- Increase settlement leverage
- Force opposing parties to confront facts directly

In some cases, simply demonstrating competence discourages unnecessary litigation.

Section IV: How Courts Actually View Pro Se Litigants

9. The Unspoken Reality

Judges are human, but bound by law.

They tend to categorize pro se litigants quickly:

1. **Unprepared and emotional** (high risk of dismissal)
2. **Overconfident and combative** (credibility problems)
3. **Prepared, focused, and respectful** (taken seriously)

Your goal is to be unmistakably in category three.

10. Professionalism Is Power

You gain credibility by:

- Dressing professionally
- Using proper titles
- Filing clean, organized pleadings
- Making concise oral arguments

You lose credibility by:

- Attacking the judge or opposing counsel
- Filing excessive motions

- Using social media language in pleadings

Professionalism is not about submission—it is about influence.

Section V: Strategic Use of Pro Se Status

11. When Pro Se Is Appropriate

Pro se representation is often suitable for:

- Procedural motions
- Discovery disputes
- Family court matters (with preparation)
- Post-judgment motions
- Administrative hearings

It may be **dangerous** in:

- Complex jury trials
- High-stakes criminal matters
- Multi-party commercial litigation

Knowing when to proceed—and when to consult counsel—is itself a form of power.

12. Limited-Scope and Hybrid Representation

You do not have to choose between *all* or *nothing*.

Many jurisdictions allow:

- Document review by attorneys
- Coaching for hearings
- Ghostwriting pleadings (with disclosure rules)

This hybrid approach combines affordability with expertise.

Section VI: Pro Se Survival Checklist

Before Filing:

- Identify the correct court and jurisdiction
- Research statutes and elements of claims
- Confirm deadlines and service rules

Before Hearings:

- Outline arguments (law first, facts second)
- Prepare exhibits with copies
- Practice concise responses

During the Case:

- Keep a litigation calendar
- Maintain a case binder
- Preserve issues for appeal

Conclusion: Power Without Illusion

Acting pro se is not about bravado.

It is about **discipline**, **education**, and **respect for the process**.

When you understand your rights, acknowledge the risks, and exercise power strategically, self-representation becomes not a disadvantage—but a calculated decision.

This book exists to give you structure where chaos is everyday, clarity where fear dominates, and power where many feel powerless.

You may stand alone—but you do not stand unarmed.

CHAPTER 14

State-by-State Differences

Introduction: One Right, Fifty Systems

The right to represent yourself exists nationwide—but **how that right is exercised, limited, and enforced varies significantly from state to state**. Court rules, judicial culture, procedural tolerance, and access to assistance differ widely. A strategy that works in one state may fail completely in another.

This chapter provides a **state-by-state practical analysis** of how pro se litigants are treated, what rules matter most, and where hidden dangers exist. It is designed to help you adapt your strategy to your jurisdiction while avoiding fatal mistakes.

Section I: Universal Rules That Apply in All States

Before examining state differences, several principles apply everywhere:

- You may represent **yourself**, but generally not others or entities
- Courts will not provide legal advice
- Procedural rules are enforceable against pro se litigants
- Judges may construe filings liberally—but not indefinitely

Liberal construction does not override jurisdictional defects, statutes of limitation, or mandatory service rules.

Section II: Categories of State Approaches to Pro Se Litigants

States generally fall into **four functional categories**. Identifying your state's category helps you predict how the court will treat you.

Category 1: Pro Se–Supportive States (Structured Assistance)

These states provide strong self-help infrastructure, standardized forms, and judicial tolerance for non-lawyers.

Common features:

- Mandatory self-help websites
- Court-approved pro se forms
- Family and civil self-help centers
- Judges accustomed to high pro se caseloads

Representative states:

- California
- Florida
- Texas
- Arizona
- Washington

Support does not equal leniency. Deadlines and service rules are still strictly enforced.

Category 2: Neutral but Rule-Strict States

These states allow self-representation but expect near-attorney-level compliance.

Common features:

- Fewer standardized forms
- Strong emphasis on civil procedure rules
- Lower tolerance for repeated errors

Representative states:

- New York

- Illinois
- Pennsylvania
- Massachusetts
- Ohio

Category 3: Restrictive or Tradition-Bound States

These states formally recognize pro se rights but maintain a rigid courtroom culture.

Common features:

- Minimal guidance from clerks
- Judges are less interventionist
- Heavy reliance on local rules

Representative states:

- Alabama
- Mississippi
- Louisiana
- Arkansas
- West Virginia

Category 4: Hybrid / Local-Rule Dominant States

In these states, outcomes depend heavily on the **county or judicial district**.

Representative states:

- Colorado
- New Jersey
- Michigan
- Minnesota
- Wisconsin

Always review local rules—statewide rules alone are insufficient.

Section III: 50-State Pro Se Differences Snapshot

Note: This chart reflects dominant practice trends, not guarantees.

A–F

- **Alabama:** Strict procedure; minimal forms; judicial discretion limited
- **Alaska:** Remote access strong; written precision critical
- **Arizona:** Robust self-help; procedural enforcement high
- **Arkansas:** Few forms; strong emphasis on service and pleading rules
- **California:** Most pro se–friendly infrastructure; high caseload tolerance
- **Colorado:** Local rules dominate; mixed judicial culture
- **Connecticut:** Guided forms available; deadlines enforced strictly
- **Delaware:** Corporate law dominance; pro se discouraged in complex matters
- **Florida:** Extensive forms; family court highly pro se-populated

G–L

- **Georgia:** Moderate support; strict motion practice
- **Hawaii:** Small-court flexibility; limited appellate tolerance
- **Idaho:** Sparse resources; strong rule compliance expected
- **Illinois:** Growing self-help centers; appellate precision required
- **Indiana:** Neutral posture; clerks provide minimal assistance
- **Iowa:** Predictable procedures; written compliance emphasized
- **Kansas:** Moderate tolerance; service errors common pitfall
- **Kentucky:** Family court flexible; civil court strict
- **Louisiana:** Civil law tradition; terminology and deadlines differ

M–R

- **Maine:** Limited infrastructure; judicial patience varies
- **Maryland:** Extensive forms; deadlines unforgiving

- **Massachusetts:** Strong rules culture; liberal construction limited
- **Michigan:** Local-rule heavy; procedural traps common
- **Minnesota:** Good online tools; strict evidentiary standards
- **Mississippi:** Conservative procedure; minimal guidance
- **Missouri:** Neutral courts; form availability inconsistent
- **Montana:** Remote filings common; precision critical
- **Nebraska:** Sparse assistance; appellate standards strict
- **Nevada:** Family law flexible; civil litigation rigid
- **New Hampshire:** Small docket flexibility; limited forms
- **New Jersey:** Strong self-help but dense rules
- **New Mexico:** Simplified forms in some divisions
- **New York:** Extensive pro se presence; high procedural expectations
- **North Carolina:** Clerk forms available; civil rules enforced
- **North Dakota:** Predictable procedure; limited tolerance
- **Ohio:** Moderate support; appellate rules critical
- **Oklahoma:** Mixed culture; local rules key
- **Oregon:** Guided interviews; written clarity emphasized
- **Pennsylvania:** Dense local rules; form availability uneven
- **Rhode Island:** Small system; judicial discretion wide

S–W

- **South Carolina:** Family court pro se common; civil strict
- **South Dakota:** Limited resources; procedural discipline required
- **Tennessee:** Forms expanding; motion practice strict
- **Texas:** Extensive self-help; deadlines are absolute
- **Utah:** Excellent online tools; strict compliance
- **Vermont:** Simplified procedures; small-court flexibility
- **Virginia:** Rule-heavy; little tolerance for error
- **Washington:** Strong pro se culture; discovery rules enforced
- **West Virginia:** Traditional courts; limited flexibility
- **Wisconsin:** Local variation significant
- **Wyoming:** Small dockets; strict procedural expectations

Section IV: High-Risk State-Specific Pitfalls

Regardless of state, the following issues disproportionately harm pro se litigants:

- **Service of process errors** (especially in strict states)
- **Local rule violations** (often unpublished or overlooked)
- **Improper motion formatting**
- **Failure to request hearings properly**
- **Missing appeal deadlines**

Section V: Strategic Adaptation by State Type

In Pro Se–Supportive States:

- Use official forms whenever available
- Avoid over-arguing—clarity beats volume

In Rule-Strict States:

- Study civil procedure rules carefully
- Mirror attorney formatting

In Restrictive States:

- Limit filings to essential motions
- Prepare extensively for hearings

In Hybrid States:

- Obtain local rules immediately
- Observe courtroom sessions if possible

Conclusion: Know the Terrain Before You Step Onto the Field

Your right to act pro se does not change across state lines—but **the terrain does**.

Successful self-representation requires adapting to the legal culture, procedural expectations, and judicial temperament of your jurisdiction.

Those who ignore state-specific differences often fail not because they are wrong—but because they are unprepared.

Knowledge of the system is power. Knowledge of *your* system is survival.

CHAPTER 15

Standing in Truth: Final Thoughts

This book was not written to promise victory, revenge, or guaranteed outcomes.

It was written to restore **clarity**, **agency**, and **truth** in a legal system that often feels overwhelming—especially for those who discover the truth *after* decisions have already been made.

Standing in truth does not mean the system will immediately agree with you. It means you now understand the terrain, the rules, and your position within it.

That knowledge changes how you move forward.

What Standing in Truth Means

Standing in truth is not about emotion. It is about alignment.

- Facts aligned with the law
- Evidence aligned with procedure
- Voice aligned with credibility

Truth without structure is ignored. Structure without truth is hollow.

This book showed you how to bring the two together.

Courts respond to truth only when it is presented correctly.

What You Now Understand

By reaching this point, you now understand realities many litigants never grasp—even after losing their case.

You know that:

- Signed documents carry legal consequences regardless of intent
- Deadlines often matter more than fairness arguments
- DNA truth alone is insufficient without a proper procedure
- Courts prioritize finality and stability
- Pro se status is a right, but discipline is required

Education does not guarantee success—but it prevents blind mistakes.

Power Without Illusion

This book never promised shortcuts.

It warned you about:

- Procedural traps
- Emotional decision-making
- State-specific differences
- Judicial limitations

False hope weakens litigants. Truth strengthens them.

Real power comes from restraint, preparation, and precision—not volume or anger.

When the System Does Not Deliver Justice

The legal system does not consistently deliver moral justice.

It delivers legal outcomes.

This distinction is painful for those who learn the truth too late—especially in matters involving identity, children, and lifelong obligations.

Standing in truth means recognizing this reality without surrendering dignity.

You are not wrong for seeking answers. You are not reckless for acting pro se when counsel is unavailable or unaffordable.

You are responsible for how you proceed next.

The Discipline of Moving Forward

Not every battle should be fought. Not every wrong can be undone. Not every case can be reopened.

Wisdom lies in knowing:

- What is legally possible
- What is strategically sound
- What is emotionally sustainable

Sometimes standing in truth means closing a chapter without closure—and choosing not to let the system define what comes next.

A Final Word to the Pro Se Litigant

Judges do not expect perfection. They expect respect, preparation, and restraint.

Credibility is built through consistency. Power is exercised through understanding.

You do not need to fight the system. You need to understand it well enough to be heard within it.

Standing in Truth, Regardless of Outcome

Outcomes matter—but they are not the sole measure of success.

Success can also mean:

- Acting with integrity
- Using available tools wisely
- Reclaiming your voice through knowledge

You now stand informed.

And that—regardless of what any order says—is something no court can take from you.

AUTHOR'S NOTES

This book exists because this issue affects **millions of men**, quietly and often invisibly.

Across the United States, hundreds of thousands of men are listed as legal fathers to children they later discover—through DNA testing or credible evidence—are not biologically theirs. Studies, court records, and child-support enforcement data consistently show that **paternity misattribution is not rare**, particularly in cases involving voluntary acknowledgments signed without counsel, hospital paperwork, or informal assurances of parentage.

Most of these men did not act irresponsibly. They trusted. They signed. They complied.

And many learned the truth only after legal obligations were already locked into place.

Once that happens, the system often shifts its focus away from biology and toward **finality, stability, and enforcement**. At that point, truth alone is no longer enough. Procedure governs everything.

This book was written for men like this.

It was also written for fathers, alleged fathers, and legal parents who sense something is wrong but do not yet understand the consequences of inaction. Silence, delay, or emotional reaction often costs more than filing the wrong document—it can cost years of financial obligation and legal identity.

I wrote this book to confront an uncomfortable reality: **the law does not automatically correct factual injustice**, especially once deadlines pass. But the law *does* provide limited pathways for those who know when and how to act.

This work is not anti-child, anti-family, or anti-court. It is pro-truth, pro-due-process, and pro-informed decision-making.

If you are reading this book, you are not alone—and you are not imagining the weight of what you discovered.

— D. Edwin Easter

www.ingramcontent.com/pod-product-compliance
Lightning Source LLC
LaVergne TN
LVHW022108200926
848481LV00003B/1103